TABLE OF C

TABLE OF CONTENTS

CURRICULUM CONNECTIONS

Basic Concepts	Lesson
Identify the four food groups and give examples of food in each group	• Food at Your Home: Home Study • Food Memory Game • Whole Group Activity: Learning about the Four Food Groups
Suggest occasions when they can choose healthy snacks	• Food at Your Home: Home Study
Describe ways to care for their teeth and prevent tooth decay	• Dental Health • Five Ways to Prevent Tooth Decay
Identify a balanced diet and apply decision-making skills to create menus for healthy meals	• Food at Your Home: Home Study • Healthy Eating Stations • A Healthy Lunch • Healthy or Unhealthy
Describe the benefits of healthy food choices	• Food at Your Home: Home Study • Healthy Eating Stations
Use decision making skills to identify healthy alternatives to drug use	• Substance Use & Abuse: Health Journal
Outline the safe use of taking medicines and employ decision-making skills to identify when and how medicine should be use	• Tips for Taking Medicine
Describe the differences between prescription and non-prescription medicine	• Substance Use & Abuse: Glossary of Terms
Identify nicotine, caffeine, and alcohol as drugs	• What Is Nicotine? • What Is Alcohol? • What Is Caffeine?
Use decision-making skills to make healthy choices about drug-use and recognize the effects of various substances on the body	• Case Studies
Recognize that there are some medicines and other substances that help the body when used properly	• Substance Use & Abuse: Health Journal • Substance Use & Abuse: Glossary of Terms
Describe simple life cycles of plants and animals, including humans	• The Life Cycle of People
Recognize that rest, food, and exercise affect growth	• Growth and Development

CURRICULUM CONNECTIONS

Basic Concepts	Lesson
Identify the major parts of the body by their proper names	• Mr. Bone's Crazy Colours • Growth and Development: Glossary of Terms
Distinguish the similarities and differences between themselves and others	• What Makes You Different?
Describe how germs are transmitted and how this relates to personal hygiene	• What Are Germs?
Identify the five senses and describe how each functions	• The Five Senses Game
Outline the basic human and animal reproductive processes	• How a Baby Is Made
Describe basic changes in growth and development from birth to childhood	• How Did Your Body Change?
Outline the potential safety risks in the home, school, and community	• The Safety Pledge • The Rules of Safety • Bicycle Safety Checklist • Bicycle Safety True or False Quiz • Bike Rules • Class Discussion Starters
Describe exploitative behaviours and the feelings associated with them	• What Is Bullying?
Identify people who can provide personal safety assistance and explain how to access them	• Who Do You Call? • What to Do in an Emergency
Identify safety rules to be followed in the home, school, and community	• Rules for School • More Rules
Explain the importance of being able to say no to exploitative behaviours and describe how to seek help	• Teaching Children About Sexual Abuse

CURRICULUM CONNECTIONS

Basic Concepts	Lesson
Explain relevant safety procedures	• Personal Safety & Injury Prevention Class Discussion Starters • Bicycle Safety Checklist • The Rules of Safety • Rules for School
Use a problem-solving process to identify ways of obtaining support for personal safety in the home, school, and community	• Bike Rules • P-A-S-T-E: A Way to Solve Problems
Learn to resolve conflict without violence	• What Would You Do? • Ways of Resolving Conflicts with Your Friends
Identify ways of helping out at home	• What Are Your Responsibilities at Home?
Identify key relationships and develop healthy ways to foster them	• Tips for Making and Keeping Friends • The Important People in Your Life
Explore what makes the student unique as a way of improving self awareness and self esteem	• The Highs and Lows in Life • The Story of Your Name • Where Do You Live? • Home Study—A Book About Me!
Explore stereotypes of boys and girls	• Stereotypes of Boys and Girls
Identify reasons for exercise	• Why Should You Exercise?
Offer activities that challenge students' fitness levels	• Games for Students • Culminating Activity: A Fitness Challenge

TEACHING TOOLS

HEALTH JOURNAL
Throughout the year, your students will complete a health journal. These journal entries will allow students to express themselves through writing or pictures. They will encourage students to express how they feel about specific health topics. You may wish for your students to share this journal with their parent(s) or guardian(s). Each unit has at least one journal entry.

For the first journal activity in the substance use and abuse unit, you may need to assist the students. The purpose of this journal is to help students understand that they don't always need to take medicine when they are sick. For instance instead, they can take a nap, go to bed early, get fresh air, and drink lots of liquids, such as juice and water.

GLOSSARY OR TERMS
Many of the units include a glossary of terms that introduces students to key terms and their definitions. You may wish to have students add other terms to these lists.

ARTICLES
In some of the units, there are short articles for your students to read with questions that follow. If your students struggle with reading, you may wish use these as oral exercises.

ASSESSMENT STRATEGIES

HEALTH JOURNAL
The Health Journal pages that students will use to express their thoughts may also be used for assessment. You might consider the students' level of skills, along with their insight, in each health journal entry.

END OF UNIT QUIZZES
The first four units have a quiz that will help determine if students have developed an understanding of the key concepts of this unit. The answers for each quiz are in the answer section at the end of the book.

HOME STUDY AND END-OF-UNIT ASSIGNMENTS
Each unit has a cumulative assignment for students to complete to reinforce concepts learned. Rubrics for the assignments have also been included.

HEALTH: PARENT LETTER

Dear Parent or Guardian:

One of the subjects your child will be studying this year is health. The following topics will be covered in the curriculum:

- healthy eating habits
- stages in development
- safety risks and practices
- substance use and abuse
- self-esteem and social relationships
- physical activities

It is important that your child extend his/her learning at home. As a result, you can help your child by encouraging healthy habits, creating a safe environment, and helping him/her develop self-esteem and a positive awareness of others.

During the year, your child may bring home various home study activities. Details of the home studies will follow. If you have any questions about these activities, please do not hesitate to contact me.

Your enthusiastic participation of our look at health is greatly appreciated.

Yours truly,

____

HEALTH JOURNAL 1

Cut and paste the pictures into the correct box.

When I feel healthy I look like.......

When I feel unhealthy I look like........

UNIT 1: HEALTHY EATING

ABOUT THIS UNIT:

In this unit, students will learn about the four food groups, learn the difference between healthy and unhealthy foods, make and eat a healthy lunch, examine who affects their food choices, and participate in a home study.

HEALTHY EATING CENTRES

The Healthy Eating Centres allow students to work with small groups rotating through five stations. Although the main focus of these stations is healthy eating, they also incorporate other subject areas, such as math, art, and language arts. Most of the stations are easy to set up; however, at STATION 1 students use math skills to calculate how much they've spent on groceries. This may require finding articles such as an empty egg container or an empty milk container and putting a price sticker on them.

Here are the products you will need with suggested prices:

A loaf of bread $1.00	1 litre of milk $1.50	1 kg. of chicken $5.50	1 bag of macaroni noodles $1.00	a box of crackers $2.00	a box of cereal $3.50
1 dozen eggs $2.00	1 can of tomato soup $0.75	1 can of apple juice $1.50	1 kg. bag of oranges $2.50	a bunch of bananas $1.25	A tin of tuna $2.00

OTHER IDEAS:

Eat Multicultural Foods:

- ✓ Collect menus from different restaurants and compare the different dishes.
- ✓ Create a multicultural recipe book.

UNIT CULMINATING ACTIVITY:

FOOD AT YOUR HOME: HOME STUDY

The students will complete three activity sheets at home. The purpose is for students to learn about the different types of foods they have at home, how to create a healthy menu, and facts about healthy food preparation. A scoring rubric can be used for assessing.

THE FOUR FOOD GROUPS

Focus:

Children will learn about the four food groups and start to categorize the types of foods they eat.

Materials Needed:

- a package of spaghetti noodles
- a loaf of bread (or a piece of bread)
- a box of cereal
- an empty orange juice carton
- a package of cheese
- an empty milk carton
- an apple
- an egg
- a jar of peanut butter
- a carrot
- a tin of tuna

Activity:

1. Explain to the students that people organize foods into four food groups. Brainstorm ideas about how they think the foods are organized.
2. You may wish to use a copy of Canada's Food Guide to explain to them the different food groups. A copy of the guide can be printed from Health Canada's Web site at http://www.hc-sc.gc.ca/hpfb-dgpsa/onpp-bppn/food_guide_rainbow_e.html
3. Post the titles of the four food groups on the board.
4. Have the students categorize the food items and place them under the appropriate titles on the board.

Follow Up Activity:

As a whole group, list the food items the students have eaten and determine into which food group they belong.

Make a separate list of foods they like to eat but are not considered healthy.

FOOD GROUP CARDS

Grain Products

Vegetables and Fruits

Milk Products

Meat and Alternatives

FOOD MEMORY GAME

Focus: *To reinforce the concept of food groups.*

Materials Needed:
(for 2 players)
Memory game cards consist of the names of the food groups and the names of different foods. There should be one copy of each of the memory game cards for each pair of students.

How to play:

1. Shuffle the cards.

2. Place the cards face down.

3. Pick up one card and then a second card. If one card is a type of food and the second card is the appropriate food group for that type of food then you have a match.

4. If you have a match, remove the cards and keep them in a pile.

5. If you don't have a match, turn both cards back down again.

6. The player with the most pairs wins.

Here are the pairs:
Tomato (vegetables & fruit)
Orange (vegetables & fruit)
Bagel (grain products)
Milk (milk products)
Cheese (milk products)
Apple juice (vegetables & fruit)
Rice (grain products)
Cereal (grain products)
Peanut butter (meat & alternatives)
Ice cream (milk products)
Ham (meat & alternatives)
Pork and beans (meat & alternatives)

FOOD MEMORY GAME CARDS

(Cut out cards)

TOMATO

VEGETABLES AND FRUIT

ORANGE

BAGEL

MILK

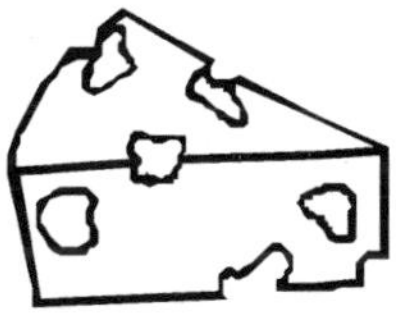

CHEESE

APPLE JUICE

GRAIN PRODUCTS

RICE

MILK PRODUCTS

GRAIN PRODUCTS

Milk PRODUCTS

FOOD MEMORY GAME CARDS

(Cut out cards)

CEREAL

GRAIN PRODUCTS

VEGETABLES AND FRUIT

VEGETABLES AND FRUIT

PEANUT BUTTER

MILK PRODUCTS

ICE CREAM

MEAT AND ALTERNATIVES

HAM

MEAT AND ALTERNATIVES

PORK AND BEANS

MEAT AND ALTERNATIVES

HEALTHY OR UNHEALTHY?

Find pictures of food in magazines. Cut and paste the pictures under the heading **HEALTHY** or under the heading **UNHEALTHY.**

Healthy Foods

Unhealthy Foods

HEALTHY EATING: HEALTH JOURNAL

Many things affect our food choices. Some of the reasons we eat the way we do are listed below. Complete the sentence for each reason.

1. Family or Guardians (the people I live with)
One way my family or guardians affect my food choices is

____

2. Culture (the country my family comes from)
One way my culture affects my food choices is

____

3. Friends (foods my friends like to eat)
One way my friends affect my food choices is

____

4. Media (food I see on TV commercials or shows)
One way the media affects my food choices is

____

CREATING A HEALTHY LUNCH

Focus:

In this activity, children will create a healthy lunch. Children will rotate through three centres.

Materials Needed:

- an English muffin for each student
- a jar of spaghetti sauce
- grated mozzarella cheese
- three slices of mushroom for each student
- two pieces of celery for each student
- a jar of cheese whiz
- enough strawberry yoghurt for each student to have some in a bowl
- a few small slices of green pepper (cut in small cubes) for each student
- small bowls
- plastic spoons and knives
- a microwave oven
- healthy drink brought by each student
- plates that can go in the microwave
- a bunch of grapes
- 10-20 raisins for each student

Activity:

The students will rotate through the three stations to make their lunch.

Station 1 **An English Muffin Pizza**	**Station 2** **Ants on a Log**	**Station 3** **Grape Dip**
You will need: • instruction cards • tomato sauce • mushrooms • English muffins (sliced in half) • the green pepper • a spoon • the mozzarella cheese	You will need: • instruction cards • the celery sticks • the cheese whiz • the raisins • plastic knives	You will need: • instruction cards • grapes • strawberry yoghurt • a small bowl

CREATING A HEALTHY LUNCH INSTRUCTION CARDS

Station 1: English Muffin Pizza

Step 1

Put two spoonfuls of sauce on your English muffin. Spread the sauce evenly.

Station 1: English Muffin Pizza

Step 2

Sprinkle the mozzarella cheese on top of the sauce.

Station 1: English Muffin Pizza

Step 3

Place a few slices of mushroom and green pepper on top.

Station 1: English Muffin Pizza

Step 4

Heat your pizza in the microwave until the cheese melts

CREATING A HEALTHY LUNCH INSTRUCTION CARDS

Station 2: Ants on a Log

Step 1

Using your knife, spread cheese whiz in the ditch of the celery sticks.

Station 2: Ants on a Log

Step 2

Place 4 or 5 raisins on the cheese whiz.

Station 3: Grape Dip

Step 1

Scoop some yoghurt into a bowl.

Station 3: Grape Dip

Step 2

Put a small handful of grapes into the bowl of yogurt and mix with your spoon.

A HEALTHY LUNCH

1. Why is the lunch you made and ate in class healthy?
2. How is it the same or different as the lunch you have every day?
3. How can you change your lunch to make it healthier?
4. The best part about making lunch was ....

HEALTHY FRUIT SALAD

Colour the fruit salad.

What is your favourite fruit?

____

HEALTHY VEGETABLES

Colour the healthy vegetables.

What are your favourite vegetables?

____

A FOOD INTERVIEW

Interview someone from another country. This person might have lived there, visited it, or just knows a lot about another country. Ask this person questions to complete the chart below.

Name of person interviewed:

____

Name of the country the person knows about:

____

Name two foods grown or produced in this country.	
Name two dishes that are popular in this country.	
Name two products from this country that you might find in your local grocery store.	
Name two products from this country that you have tasted before. If you haven't eaten anything from this country, pick two items that you think you'd like to try.	
What is one fact that you found interesting from interviewing this person?	

HEALTHY EATING STATION INSTRUCTION CARDS

HEALTHY EATING STATION 1

Pretend you are at a grocery store.

Here is the list of what you need to buy.

- 1 loaf of bread
- 1 dozen eggs
- 1 bag of macaroni noodles
- 1 can of tomato soup
- a box of crackers
- a box of cereal
- a bunch of bananas
- 1 kg. bag of oranges
- 1 kg. of chicken
- 1 litre of milk
- 1 can of apple juice

Look at the prices of the groceries at the station.
You only have $5.00 to buy things from the list.
Decide what things you would not buy in order not to run out of money.
What is your reason for not buying this?
Use a calculator.

HEATHLY EATING STATION 2

Pretend you own a restaurant. You have decided to have a healthy menu at your restaurant. Create a menu with at least three items for each heading. Here are the headings your menu should have:

1. **STARTERS**

2. **MAIN COURSE**

3. **DESSERTS**

4. **DRINKS**

HEALTHY EATING STATION INSTRUCTION CARDS

HEATHLY EATING STATION 3

The Canadian Government has hired you to create a healthy eating poster. This poster should have a slogan that encourages people to eat healthy foods. Your poster should:

- Have pictures.
- Information people about why they need to eat healthy food.
- Have clear and easy to read writing.
- Be as neat as possible!

HEATHLY EATING STATION 4

Create a healthy eating cheer. You will share this cheer with your classmates. Here is an example of a healthy eating cheer:

Banana, banana, bananas and grapes.
Together I think they really taste great!
Mix in an orange and an apple too.
Grapefruit. Watermelon. Fruit that's blue.
It'll taste great in a salad for two.
It'll taste great on a summer afternoon!

Now it's your turn.

HEALTHY EATING STATION INSTRUCTION CARDS

HEATHLY EATING STATION 5

Below is a list of what different people have eaten in a meal. None of these meals is healthy. For each person change something to make his or her meal healthier.

Meal 1—Amhed

Amhed had the following for breakfast:

- 2 donuts
- 2 cans of soda pop

Meal 2—Lorna

Lorna had the following for lunch:

- half a tuna sandwich
- five cookies
- a chocolate bar
- a bag of chips
- a banana
- a can of soda pop

Meal 3—Edwardo

Edwardo had the following for dinner:

- one hamburger from a fast-food restaurant
- one serving of extra large French fries
- one ice-cream sundae
- one can of pop

PARENT LETTER

FOOD AT YOUR HOME: HOME STUDY

Dear Parents and Guardians:

As part of our study of food and healthy eating, we would like your child to participate in a home study. This study will involve looking at food in your home, creating healthy menus, and learning about the care you take when preparing food.

This is an opportunity for you to discuss things such as why you wash fruit and vegetables before eating them, or why you keep meat frozen. During this study, you may also invite your child work with you in the kitchen, explaining the importance of why we keep a kitchen clean.

This home study will

- allow students to examine the different types of healthy foods they have at home
- teach students how to create a healthy menu
- learn facts about food preparation

For this study, your child will need to complete three handouts. Your assistance in working with your child on this home study is appreciated.

Yours truly,

____

FOOD AT YOUR HOME: HOME STUDY

Go on a scavenger hunt around your home and fill out this chart.

Name a food that is a fruit.	Name a food that comes in a tin.	Name a food that belongs in the meat and alternative group.	Name a food that you store in the fridge.
Name a food that is in your freezer.	Name a food that is red.	Name a food that is a vegetable.	Name a food that you like to eat for breakfast.
Name an item in your fridge that you drink.	Name a food item that you put on another food item to help with taste.	Name a food that is from the grain products group.	Name a food that must be cooked before you can eat it.
Name a food that you might spread on bread.	Name a food that is from the milk products group.	Name a food that is green.	Name a food that comes in a box or a bag.

FOOD AT YOUR HOME: HOME STUDY

Choose three items to complete each group.

Name three healthy snacks you eat at home.
1.
2.
3.

Name three things your parents or guardians do before preparing food, while preparing food, or after preparing food to make sure the food and kitchen is clean.
1.
2.
3.

Name three benefits of eating healthy foods.
1.
2.
3.

FOOD IN YOUR HOME: HOME STUDY

Plan a healthy breakfast, lunch, and dinner for your family to eat.

Include everything that you would eat in the meal.

Have you covered the four food groups? After each meal explain what makes it healthy.

BREAKFAST

What makes this breakfast healthy?

____

____

LUNCH

What makes this lunch healthy?

____

____

DINNER

What makes this dinner healthy?

____

____

FOOD IN YOUR HOME
HOME STUDY SCORING RUBRIC

CRITERIA	LEVEL 1	LEVEL 2	LEVEL 3	LEVEL 4
Clarity of Ideas	- very difficult to understand information on the activity sheets	- difficult to understand information on the activity sheets	- the information on the activity sheets is clear and understandable	- the information on the activity sheets is extremely clear and understandable
Organization	- had lots of difficulty organizing the material in the graphic organizers and spaces provided.	- had some difficulty organizing the material in the graphic organizers and spaces provided.	- had no difficulty organizing the material in the graphic organizers and spaces provided.	- organized the information using the graphic organizers and space providers in an exceptional manner
Proofreading	- so many language errors it is difficult to understand text	- many language errors that sometimes makes it difficult to understand text	- some language errors, but errors don't take away from meaning	- very few language errors
Level of Assistance (information required from parents)	- ample adult assistance was required	- some adult assistance was required	- little adult assistance was required	- no adult assistance was required

ADDITIONAL COMMENTS:

____

____

____

HEALTHY EATING QUIZ

Put a check mark beside the healthy foods.

1. ___ Chocolate bar 	2. ___ Ham sandwich 
3. ___ Ice cream sundae 	4. ___ Glass of milk 
5. ___ An egg 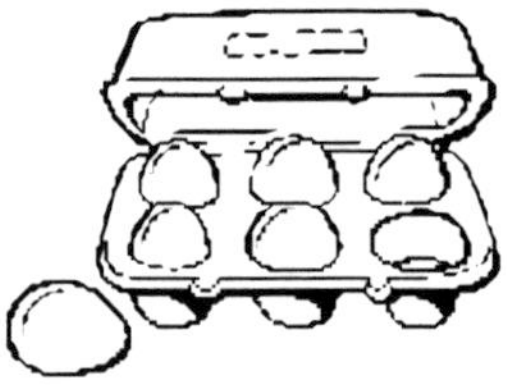	6. ___ Potato chips 
7. ___ A banana 	8. ___ A piece of bread 
9. ___ A carrot 	10. ___ French fries 
11. ___ Fish 	12. ___ A piece of cake 

HEALTHY EATING

Colour the picture. Make a list of foods that would make a healthy supper.

DENTAL HEALTH

WHAT CAUSES CAVITIES?

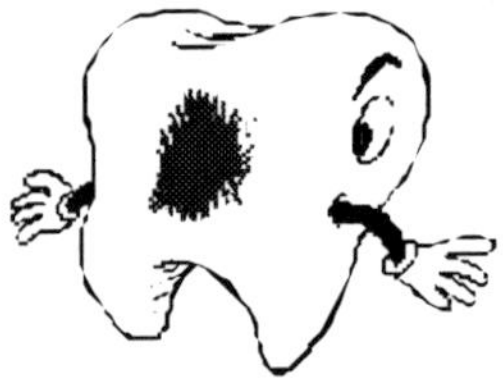

Bacteria or little living organisms are on your teeth, gums, lips, and tongue. This is normal. Some bacteria can cause damage, and some can be helpful.

Certain kinds of bacteria can attach themselves to the enamel that covers your teeth. If they're not taken away, they grow until a colony forms. The bacteria colony looks like a whitish film on the tooth. This film is called plaque, and it's what causes cavities. Fluoride helps prevent cavities. Fluoride can be found in many things. It can be in the water we drink and the food we eat. Scientists noted that children, who lived in places where fluoride occurred naturally in the water, had fewer dental cavities.

Your body uses fluoride to make stronger enamel on your teeth, so using toothpaste with fluoride in it is a good idea!

Learn what fluoride can do for you by trying this experiment.

Materials:

1. 1 bottle of Fluoride rinse solution (you can get this from your dentist, a dental supply company and some pharmacies)
2. 1 bottle of white vinegar
3. 2 eggs
4. 3 containers

This is what to do:

1. Put some Fluoride rinse solution into one of the containers.
2. Put an egg in the solution.
3. Soak the egg for five minutes.
4. Take out the egg.
5. Pour vinegar into the remaining two containers.
6. Put the egg that has been treated with the Fluoride into one container of vinegar.
7. Put the untreated egg in the other container of vinegar.

What happens: Why do you think one egg bubbles?

DENTAL HEALTH

GROWTH & DEVELOPMENT OF TEETH

"Baby" teeth usually begin to appear in infants between six and ten months of age. The front middle teeth (Central Incisors) usually come in first. By the time a child is three years old, most of the "baby" teeth are grown in.

At around seven years old, the baby teeth start to fall out and permanent teeth begin to replace them. By twenty-one, most adults have all of their permanent teeth.

WHY BRUSH YOUR TEETH?

Brushing your teeth is the best way to take plaque off of your teeth. Plaque causes cavities.

Brushing your teeth with a soft brush will help to remove the plaque. Brushing with a stiff brush or brushing too hard can cause damage to your gums. You should brush your teeth in a gentle circular motion to massage your gums and get into all the surfaces of your teeth.

Most people think they brush their teeth long enough, but they usually only brush for half a minute or so. A good brushing should last about two to three minutes!

Remember flossing is as important as brushing. Floss gets to the areas in between teeth that brushes cannot reach.

FIVE WAYS TO PREVENT TOOTH DECAY

1. Visit your dentist regularly. Your dentist can to see hidden problems you can't.

2. Floss your teeth everyday. Dental floss can reach areas that your toothbrush can't.

3. Eat a well-balanced diet. Try not to snack between meals, especially on sticky, sweet things like candy.

4. Keep an eye on your gums. Puffy, red or sore gums or gums that bleed and bad breath are signs that you need to see your dentist.

5. Brush your teeth carefully after every meal. Remember, to do a good job, it takes 2 to 3 minutes of brushing in small circles.

HEALTHY EATING CERTIFICATE

Congratulations!

____

You have completed the Healthy Eating unit.

You did "grape" work!

Reflection Journal

The part I liked best about the healthy eating unit was........

____

Two things I learned ....

1. ______________________________

2. ______________________________

UNIT 2: SUBSTANCE USE & ABUSE

In this unit, students will learn the difference between prescription and non-prescription drugs, tips for taking medicine, understand what is caffeine, nicotine, alcohol, and other illegal drugs, explain how they would respond to certain situations, think of why people take drugs, and create a poster encouraging people to quit smoking.

UNIT OVERVIEW:

During this unit, the teacher may want to invite a nurse, doctor, or other health care professional into the classroom to discuss issues such as how to use medicine properly, rules for taking medicine, and healthy alternatives to drug use.

You may also want to bring in household products, such as hair spray and cleaning products, and go over what the different warning symbols represent.

ASSESSMENT STRATEGIES:

POSTER ASSIGNMENT:

In the Substance Use and Abuse Unit, the students will create a poster to encourage smokers to quit smoking. Before they create their poster, you may wish to brainstorm as a class reasons why people should quit smoking. A scoring rubric has been provided for your use in assessing the posters.

SUBSTANCE USE & ABUSE: HEALTH JOURNAL

I take medicine when I am

____.

Instead of taking medicine, here are four things I could do to get well.

1.____

____

2.____

____

3.____

____

4.____

____

SUBSTANCE USE & ABUSE GLOSSARY OF TERMS

DRUG:	Substances used by a person that affect his or her body. Sometimes a drug is used as medicine to help the body; sometimes a drug is used in a harmful way and damages the body.
MEDICINE:	Substances used to treat diseases and illnesses.
PRESCRIPTION DRUGS:	These are drugs that are prescribed or ordered by a doctor. They are purchased at a pharmacy or drug store.
NON-PRESCRIPTION DRUGS:	These are drugs that a person can get without a doctor's prescription. They are purchased at a pharmacy or drug store.

TIPS FOR TAKING MEDICINE

1. Always ask an adult for assistance.

2. Read the label carefully and follow the instructions.

3. Don't take more medicine than the label tells you to take.

4. Make sure you understand why you are taking the medicine and what it should do for your body.

5. If you have a strange reaction to the medicine, make sure you tell an adult immediately.

6. If the medicine doesn't do what it is supposed to do, you may want to see a doctor.

7. Don't be afraid to ask questions.

HARMFUL AND BAD SIGNS

Sometimes products like household cleaners are bad or have bad substances in them. If a product has a picture of poison on it, then you should not touch or taste this product. Remember to stay safe and stay away from cleaning products.

WHAT IS CAFFEINE?

Caffeine is a drug found in coffee beans, tea-leaves, cacao, and cola nuts. Cacao is used to make chocolate. Coffee beans are used to make coffee. Cola nuts are used to make pop. Caffeine helps make people feel more awake. This is why many adults begin their day with a cup of coffee.

Lots of caffeine may make a person's heart pump faster and they may breathe faster. Caffeine can also make people go to the bathroom a lot.

Caffeine Is a Drug

Caffeine is a legal drug. Like any drug, it can be addictive. Being addicted to caffeine isn't as harmful as being addicted to illegal drugs.

Why Too Much Caffeine Is Bad for You

Some people, who drink or eat a lot of things with caffeine in them, can get headaches and stomachaches when the caffeine is taken away. Some people can feel sleepy or grumpy if they don't have this drug.

Too much caffeine can cause some people to get shaky and can also prevent sleep. This is why you shouldn't have pop before going to bed.

Caffeine makes it difficult for your body to get the right amount of water needed to function. So if you are thirsty, it's better to drink water, milk, or juice instead of cola, since water, milk and juice are all caffeine-free.

Try to Avoid Too Much Caffeine

Try to avoid having too much caffeine. When you get older, you may want to drink decaffeinated coffee or tea. Decaffeinated means that most of the caffeine has been removed from these beverages. Also, clear pop like 7-Up, Sprite, or Ginger Ale does not have caffeine.

So the next time you see an adult who is in a grumpy mood in the morning, don't assume they got out of the wrong side of bed. This person might be missing their morning caffeine!

WHAT IS CAFFEINE?

1. Fill in the blanks using the information from the reading and the word box.

A. Caffeine is a drug found in ________________,

________________, ________________, and ________________.

B. Caffeine helps make people more ________________.

C. Lots of caffeine may make a person's ________________ pump

faster and they may ________________ faster.

D. Caffeine can also make ________________ go to the bathroom.

Words

people, coffee beans, cacao,

breathe, awake, tea-leaves, heart, cola nuts

2. Name two ways caffeine affects the body.

A.____

B. ____

3. What might happen to a person who is addicted to caffeine if he or she doesn't have caffeine?

____

4. List 3 other things you can drink that do not contain caffeine.

A. ______________ B. ________________ C. ______________

WHAT IS NICOTINE?

Some people think smoking cigarettes is a bad habit. Smoking cigarettes causes people to have bad breath, yellow skin, horrible coughs, and can even lead to deadly diseases, such as cancer. Buying cigarettes also costs people lots of money.

Tobacco is a plant smoked in cigarettes. Tobacco contains nicotine. Nicotine is very addictive. Although nicotine causes a good feeling in the body, this feeling lasts only a short time. People who smoke also have a higher chance of getting colds and pneumonia. Since smoking affects our lungs, smokers often find it difficult to participate in sports.

Many people start smoking as young as 10 or 11 years of age. The number one reason people give for starting to smoke is because their friends talked them into it. Most smokers will tell you that they want to quit. However, nicotine is such an addictive drug that it is very difficult for most smokers to stop. Many people say the best way to stop smoking is to make sure you never start in the first place!

WHAT IS ALCOHOL?

Like nicotine and caffeine, alcohol is a legal drug. However, teenagers, especially, often abuse this drug. Alcohol is found in beer, wine, and some other beverages.

Alcohol is a depressant, meaning it slows down your brain. Alcohol has both short-term and long-term side effects. If a person has a few drinks, he/she may have a short-term effect such as slurred speech, a loss of balance, and blurry vision. People who drink too much at one time may throw up or pass out. Because alcohol prevents messages from properly getting to the brain, it is important a person doesn't drive after drinking.

Some people become addicted to alcohol and may become alcoholics. Alcoholism is a disease that is difficult to overcome and alcoholics are people who crave and depend on alcohol. Alcoholics may suffer from the long-term affects of alcohol, which are permanent nerve, liver, or brain damage or serious diseases like cancer of the stomach.

After reading the information about nicotine and alcohol, complete the chart.

COMPARING NICOTINE & ALCOHOL

	Nicotine	Alcohol
What is it?		
What are the short-term affects of this drug?		
What are the long-term affects of this drug?		

ILLEGAL DRUGS

Some drugs are illegal. In the chart below, learn about three such illegal drugs.

What is it?	**Marijuana**	**Heroin**	**Cocaine**
	This is the most used illegal drug in Canada. It comes from the shredded leaves of the hemp plant.	This is a very addictive drug that comes from a flower that grows in Asia and South America	This is a very addictive drug that is a white powder that comes from the dried leaves of a coca plant.
Other names for this drug.	This drug is sometimes called pot, weed, or grass.	This drug is sometimes called smack, big H, or black tar.	This drug is sometimes called coke or snow.
Why this drug is bad for you?	This drug is addictive. It can raise your heart beat, make you hungry, give you red eyes, and make you sleepy. It is tough on your lungs. This drug is often called the 'gate-way' drug because it can lead people to try more harmful drugs.	This is a highly addictive drug. Too much of it can cause an overdose and kill a person. If an addicted person tries to stop taking this drug, he or she goes into withdrawal and can have panic attacks, severe chills, and the shakes.	This is a very, very addictive drug. It is so dangerous that just using it once could cause a heart attack and kill a person. Most people get addicted to this drug after trying it only once. This drug provides people with an intense feeling of power and energy.

CASE STUDIES
WHAT WOULD YOU DO?

Read the following situations.
Tell what you would do.

1. A friend stole a cigarette from his grandfather. He wants you to smoke it with him. What would you do?

   ____

   ____

   ____

2. You are at a family picnic and you notice your uncle has had a few alcoholic drinks. When it is time to go home, your Mom tells you that your uncle will be driving you. She doesn't know that he has been drinking alcohol. What would you do?

   ____

   ____

   ____

3. You have a two-year-old baby brother. He is in the bathroom playing with cleaning solutions that have a poison symbol on the label. What would you do?

   ____

   ____

   ____

SUBSTANCE USE & ABUSE HEALTH JOURNAL

1. Sometimes people need to take drugs. What is a good reason why people should take drugs?

____

____

2. Sometimes drugs are bad for you. What is a bad reason people take drugs?

____

____

3. List one drug that is a legal drug and one drug that is an illegal drug.

Legal Drug: ____________________

Illegal Drug: ____________________

SUBSTANCE USE & ABUSE POSTER ASSIGNMENT

You are going to make a poster that encourages people to quit smoking. Before making your poster, think of five reasons why people should quit smoking.

1. ______________________________

2. ______________________________

3. ______________________________

4. ______________________________

5. ______________________________

Your poster should have:

- at least one picture.
- a catchy slogan that gives people one reason why they should quit smoking.
- neat, easy to read printing.

SUBSTANCE USE & ABUSE

Poster Assignment: Scoring Rubric

CRITERIA	LEVEL 1	LEVEL 2	LEVEL 3	LEVEL 4
Knowledge	- does not provide a reason to quit smoking	- provides a reason to quit smoking, but the reason lacks knowledge of the issue	- provides a good reason to quit smoking	- provides an excellent and insightful reason to quit smoking
Clarity of Ideas	- very difficult to understand information on poster	- difficult to understand information on poster	- the information on the poster is clear and understandable	- the information on the poster is extremely clear and understandable
Communication	- visuals have no connection to the message of the poster	- visuals have a limited connection to the message of the poster	- visuals have a good connection to the message of the poster	- visuals have an excellent connection to the message of the poster
Proofreading	- so many language errors it is difficult to understand text	- lots of language errors that sometimes makes it difficult to understand text	- some language errors, but errors don't take away from meaning	- very few language errors

Additional Comments

____

____

SUBSTANCE USE & ABUSE
TRUE OR FALSE QUIZ

Circle TRUE or FALSE.

1. Nicotine is an illegal drug.	TRUE or FALSE
2. You should always ask an adult before you take any medicine.	TRUE or FALSE
3. A prescription drug is ordered by a doctor.	TRUE or FALSE
4. 7-Up, water, and milk all contain high levels of caffeine.	TRUE or FALSE
5. Alcoholics are people who crave and depend on alcohol.	TRUE or FALSE
6.Marijuana is an illegal drug in Canada.	TRUE or FALSE
7. Cocaine is not very addictive.	TRUE or FALSE
8. A long-term effect of smoking is lung cancer.	TRUE or FALSE
9. All drugs are bad for people.	TRUE or FALSE
10. The best way to quit smoking is not to start in the first place.	TRUE or FALSE

SUBSTANCE USE & ABUSE CERTIFICATE

Congratulations!

____

You have completed
the Substance Use and Abuse unit.

Great Work!

Substance Use & Abuse **Name**__________________

Reflection Journal

The part I liked best about the substance use and abuse unit was........

____

Two things I learned ....

1. ______________________________________

2. ______________________________________

UNIT 3:
GROWTH AND DEVELOPMENT

In this unit, students will examine what makes them physically unique. They will learn how to take care of their bodies; about the five senses; germs; understand the life cycle of people and how babies are made. They will examine how their bodies have changed from when they were babies.

OVERVIEW:

During this unit teachers should be sensitive to the fact that some students may be overweight or have physical disabilities that could result in them feeling awkward about discussing their bodies.

In a world where many teens and adults suffer from weight disorders that range from obesity to anorexia and bulimia, teachers may decide not to stress weight in this unit. The only time weight is mentioned is on the activity sheet "What Makes You Different?" Teachers may decide comparing weight is inappropriate in class. In this case teachers can decide to tell the students a scale is unavailable in the classroom and the class will not be required to answer the question "What is your weight?"

For students who struggle with reading, teachers may wish to read the statements from the true and false quiz or the articles. Students may then answer the questions after hearing them.

CULMINATING ACTIVITY

GROWTH AND DEVELOPMENT: HOME STUDY

In this assignment, students will complete a series of worksheets. They will examine a five-day period of their own sleeping habits and what they do to grow healthy during the day.

A scoring rubric can be used for assessing. Teachers may wish to incorporate math skills and other enrichment activities. For example, teachers may wish to introduce the students to bar graphs and have them graph the number of hours they sleep each day.

GROWTH AND DEVELOPMENT GLOSSARY OF TERMS

BLOOD	carries oxygen and other nutrients to the places in your body that need them.
BONES	give our bodies structure and help protect our inner organs.
BRAIN	is like a computer. The human brain allows people to think, makes the rest of the body function, and gives us our memories.
HEART	is a muscle located a little to the left of the middle of your chest. Its main job is to pump blood around your body.
MUSCLES	are tissues that help your body operate properly. Your muscles do many jobs in your body. For example, they keep your heart beating, they help you move, and they allow you to smile.
SKIN	is the protective covering on your body. It protects your insides and also helps keep you warm.

GROWTH AND DEVELOPMENT HEALTH JOURNAL

Use as many words as you can to describe your body.

Draw a self portrait.

I am special because ______________________________

____

GROWTH AND DEVELOPMENT

In order to grow big and tall you need:

- sleep
- exercise
- healthy food
- water

To take care of yourself you must:

- wash and bathe regularly
- wear clean clothes
- brush your teeth
- comb your hair

THE LIFE CYCLE OF PEOPLE

A life cycle is the stages of growth and death that living things go through. As a human, we go through stages of growth and development, until one day we die.

Think about the stages a human goes through. Look at the words that describe the stages of the human life cycle. Number the stages in the order you think they happen.

___ Toddler ___ Adult ___ Baby in the womb

___ Birth ___ Young child ___ Teenager

___ Death ___ Newborn baby

Cut out the pictures. On another piece of paper put them in order of the human life cycle.

MR. BONE'S CRAZY COLOURS

Read, label, and colour

- Colour the arms RED.
- Colour the head YELLOW.
- Colour the hands BLACK.
- Colour the legs BLUE.
- Colour the feet ORANGE.
- Colour the body GREEN.

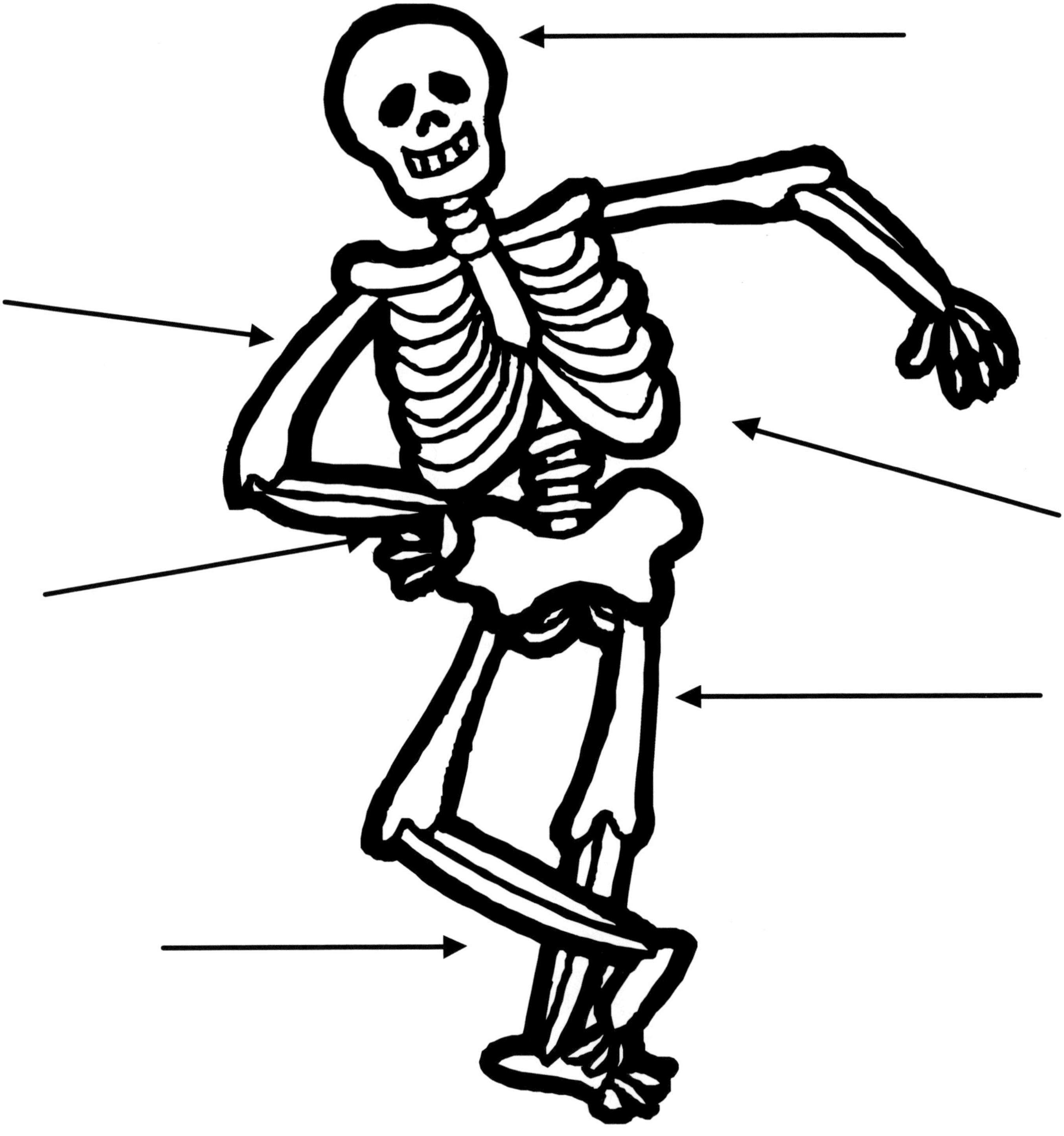

INTERESTING FACTS ABOUT YOUR BODY

Did you know that every minute of the day you lose between 30,000 and 40,000 dead skin cells? This means you lose about 4.5 kilograms of skin cells every year!

Did you know that adults have 206 bones in their bodies and 650 muscles?

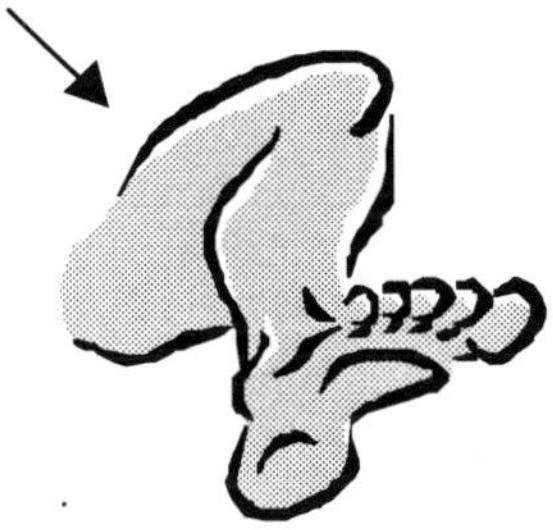

Did you know the longest bone in your body is the femur? The femur is the bone in your leg that goes from your pelvis to your knee.

Did you know that, for its size, the tongue is the strongest muscle in your body?

Did you know that your skin is your body's biggest organ? If you spread your skin out like a blanket, it would be 1.8 square meters.

Did you know when you sneeze that you send particles out of your nose at a speed of up to 160 kilometers an hour?

Did you know that half of your body weight is made up of muscle? If you weigh 30 kilograms, then 15 kilograms of your body is muscle.

WHAT MAKES YOU DIFFERENT?

Everyone is different in some way. We all have different bodies. Pick a partner. Use the chart below to show you how you and your partner are the same and how you are different.

	Your name ____________	**Your partner's name** ____________
What is your height?		
What is your gender?		
What is your skin colour?		
What is your hair colour?		
What is your eye colour?		
What is your weight?		
What is your hair length?		
How are you different?		
How are you similar?		

THE FIVE SENSES GAME

INSTRUCTIONS:

Explain to the students that you will read them a series of clues. After each clue, ask for guesses as to what they think the object is.

OBJECT 1

This object looks white and is very small.
No two of these ever look the same.
It is silent even when you listen hard.
It has no smell.
It has no taste.
It is very cold.
What is it?
(Answer— a snow flake)

OBJECT 2

This object looks red, yellow, and orange.
It seems to move around a lot.
It makes crackling sounds.
If you could taste this object, it would have no taste.
You should never touch this object because it would burn your skin.
This object might smell smoky.
What is it?
(Answer— fire)

OBJECT 3

This object grows on trees.
It is long and yellow.
When you touch it, it can be hard or soft.
It tastes good.
It smells sweet.
It can be taken apart.
What is it?
(Answer – banana)

Have students generate their own riddles.

WHAT ARE GERMS?

Germs are tiny, invisible, living things that sometimes cause diseases. They are so small that you can only see them with a microscope. Two types of germs are bacteria and viruses.

Bacteria

Bacteria get food from their environments in order to survive. In some cases, these environments are the human body. Bacteria can be both good and bad for people. Good bacteria help us digest our food. Bad bacteria can cause infections like strep throat, cavities, or pneumonia. Bacteria can live anywhere, so it is important to wash your hands, especially before eating, and after going to the bathroom!

Viruses

When viruses are inside people's bodies, they can make them sick. Viruses cause illnesses like measles, chicken pox, and the flu. Viruses are not able to live outside the body.

How Do Germs Travel?

Germs can move easily. They can move through the air when people sneeze or cough. They can also be passed through spit, sweat, and blood. If Samantha has a cold and shakes hands with Jon, she might pass along the cold to Jon. When Jon touches his mouth or nose, he may get the germs from Samantha.

How Do You Stay Away from Germs?

The best way to protect yourself from germs is to wash your hands with soap and warm water. After you use the washroom, before you handle or eat food, and after you sneeze or cough, you should always wash your hands. To protect other people from your germs, always cover your mouth when you cough or sneeze.

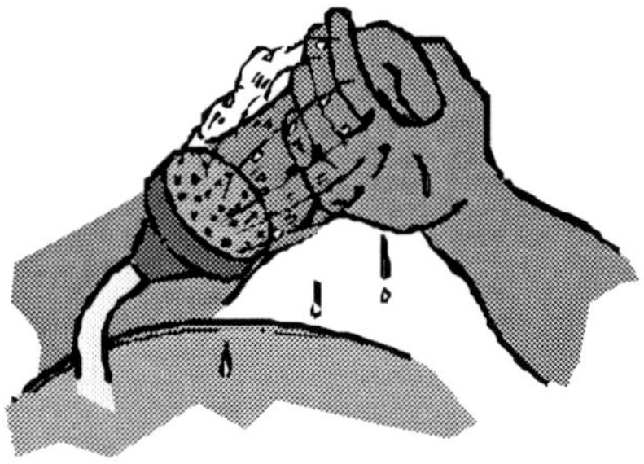

QUESTIONS
WHAT ARE GERMS?

1. What are germs?

____

2. What are two types of germs?

____

3. What are some illnesses caused by bacteria?

____

4. What are some illnesses caused by viruses?

____

5. What is one thing that makes bacteria different from viruses?

____

6. What can you do to protect yourself from germs?

____

HOW DID YOUR BODY CHANGE?

As you grew from a baby to a child, your body changed.

Complete the chart below by describing how your body changed for each body part mentioned.

Body Part	Baby	Child
Teeth		
Hair		
Height		
Weight		
Eye sight		
Hands and Feet		

HOW A BABY IS MADE

1. Once a month, a woman releases an egg from a place inside her body called the ovaries.

2. In order for a woman to become pregnant, after the egg leaves the ovaries, it must connect with a the sperm that the man releases inside the woman's body.

3. The man's penis enters the woman's vagina.

4. Inside the vagina, the penis releases millions of sperm.

5. Once the sperm and egg unite, they move to a place in the woman's body called the uterus. This becomes the baby's home for nine months. This is where the baby grows before becoming born.

GROWTH AND DEVELOPMENT HOME STUDY

Dear Parents and Guardians:

As part of our growth and development unit, your child will participate in a home study. In class, we have discussed four things that your child needs in order to become big, strong, and healthy. These are sleep, exercise, healthy food, and water. The purpose of this home study is for your child to explore how these four areas affect his/her own growth and development.

In this home study, your child will complete three handouts that have him/her examine his/her sleeping habits and daily habits. Please help your child complete these worksheets.

Although this home study is part of our health program, it also allows your child to improve his/her math and language arts skills.

If you have any questions about this home study, please don't hesitate to contact me.

Sincerely,

____

HOW MUCH SLEEP DO YOU GET EACH NIGHT?

To grow healthy, you must get lots of sleep. Keep track of when you go to bed and when you wake up.
Use these 5 sheets to help track this information.

After five days, complete the "Examine Your Sleeping Habits Journal."

Date ____________________________

What time did you go to bed?

____

Show it on the clock.

What time did you wake up?

____

Show it on the clock.

How many hours of sleep did you get?

____

EXAMINE YOUR DAILY HABITS

What do you do during the day to help you grow big and strong? This might include food you eat, water, fresh air, exercise, and playing with your friends. Keep track of what you do each day over a five day period.

DAY 1	
DAY 2	
DAY 3	
DAY 4	
DAY 5	

What are your good daily habits that help you grow big and strong?

____

____

What can you do to improve your daily habits?

____

____

EXAMINE YOUR SLEEPING HABITS JOURNAL

Look at the number of hours you sleep each night. Do you think you get enough sleep at night? Explain your thinking.

____

____

____

Read the questions.
To answer the questions, circle **NEVER**, **SOMETIMES**, or **OFTEN**.

1. Do you wake up in the night and have trouble getting back to sleep? NEVER SOMETIMES OFTEN
2. Do you have trouble falling asleep once you go to bed? NEVER SOMETIMES OFTEN
3. Do you have nightmares or bad dreams? NEVER SOMETIMES OFTEN
4. Do you hear noises inside or outside your room that keep you up at night? NEVER SOMETIMES OFTEN
5. Do you share a bedroom with someone or a pet who wakes you up at night? NEVER SOMETIMES OFTEN

GROWTH AND DEVELOPMENT
HOME STUDY RUBRIC

CRITERIA	LEVEL 1	LEVEL 2	LEVEL 3	LEVEL 4
Completion of Assignment	- did not complete any of the worksheets that examined their sleep habits and daily habits	- only completed one of the worksheets that examined their sleep habits and daily habits	- only completed two of the worksheets that examined their sleep habits and daily habits	- completed all three of the worksheets that examined their sleep habits and healthy habits
Organization	- had lots of difficulty writing the material in the graphic organizers and charts and completing the journal	- had some difficulty writing the material in the graphic organizers and charts and completing the journal	- had no difficulty writing the material in the graphic organizers and charts and completing the journal	- wrote the material in the graphic organizers and charts and completed the journal in a superb manner
Proofreading	- so many language errors it is difficult to understand text	- lots of language errors that sometimes makes it difficult to understand text	- some language errors, but errors don't take away from meaning	- very few language errors
Level of Assistance (information required from parents)	- lots of adult assistance was required	- some adult assistance was required	- little adult assistance was required	- no adult assistance was required

ADDITIONAL COMMENTS

GROWTH AND DEVELOPMENT TRUE OR FALSE QUIZ

Read the sentence. Circle **TRUE** or **FALSE**

1. A person needs sleep, exercise, healthy food, and water to grow big and strong.	TRUE or FALSE
2. The purpose of skin is to help blood flow to the heart.	TRUE or FALSE
3. Bones help protect your inner organs.	TRUE or FALSE
4. The five senses are the sense of sight, the sense of hearing, the sense of smell, the sense of taste, and the sense of touch.	TRUE or FALSE
5. Germs are only passed from one person to another by shaking hands.	TRUE or FALSE
6. One of the best ways to protect yourself from germs to wash your hands.	TRUE or FALSE
7. Two types of germs are bacteria and viruses.	TRUE or FALSE
8. People need healthy foods to help them grow.	TRUE or FALSE
9. A teenager is the stage before a toddler in the stages of the life cycle.	TRUE or FALSE
10. To take care of yourself, you should brush your teeth, comb your air, and bathe regularly.	TRUE or FALSE

GROWTH AND DEVELOPMENT CERTIFICATE

Congratulations!

____

You have completed
the Growth and Development unit.

Great Work!

Growth and Development
Reflection Journal

The part I liked best about the growth and development unit was........

____

Two things I learned ....

1. ______________________________

2. ______________________________

UNIT 4: PERSONAL SAFETY & INJURY PREVENTION

In this unit, students will learn about fire safety, bicycle safety, and rules at school. They will examine inappropriate touching, who to call in an emergency, and what bullying is. Discussions will be encouraged on how to help in certain situations. Students will create a safety bookmark.

UNIT OVERVIEW:

Teachers may wish to call the local fire department and ask a fire fighter to visit the class to discuss fire safety; or have the local police department visit and talk about safety.

Representatives from Child Find Canada are available. See their site at:

http://www.childfind.ca

Child Find Canada offers fingerprinting clinics as well as teaching children skills to protect themselves and developing an awareness of missing children.

CULMINATING ACTIVITY

SAFETY BOOKMARK

In this unit, students will create a bookmark with two safety rules based on information learned in the unit. A rubric is included to help with marking the bookmark.

PERSONAL SAFETY & INJURY PREVENTION

Class Discussion Starters

These discussion starters about safety risks at home, school, and in the community may be used to develop KWL charts.

1. What might happen if you play with matches or a lighter?

2. What might happen to you if you race across the street without looking both ways?

3. If you have a baby brother or sister, what toys should you keep away from them?

4. What should you wear on a boat for safety?

5. If you see lightening, why shouldn't you go swimming?

6. How long should you wait after a meal before swimming? Why do you need to wait?

7. Why should you wear a seat belt in a car?

8. What can you do at a pool or near a lake to make sure you are safe?

9. What would you do if there were a fire in your home?

10. Why shouldn't you play in tunnels in snow banks or build snow forts with high walls?

11. What would you do if a stranger approached you and asked you to go into their car?

12. Why should you never play with electrical outlets?

PERSONAL SAFETY & INJURY PREVENTION HEALTH JOURNAL

Fire safety is very important. Unfortunately many people die or lose their homes in fires every year. Below are pictures of items. Put a check mark on the picture of things people should have in their homes to help prevent or protect them in a fire.

 stove	 matches	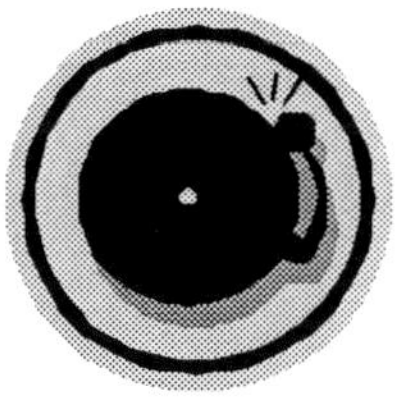 fire alarm
 telephone	 fire extinguisher	 television
 car	 smoke detector	 barbecue
 blanket	 firefighter	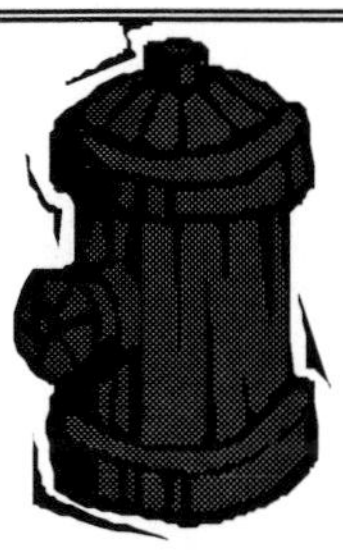 fire hydrant

RULES FOR SCHOOL

Divide the class into four groups. Give each group one of the following cards, along with a piece of chart paper and a marker. Have the students create as many rules as possible. After they have completed this assignment, have them share the rules with the rest of the class.

GROUP 1–RULES FOR GYM CLASS

Think of as many rules as you can that should be followed in gym class.

GROUP 2–RULES FOR THE SCHOOLYARD

Think of as many rules as you can that should be followed in the schoolyard.

GROUP 3–RULES FOR THE SCHOOL BUS

Think of as many rules as you can that should be followed in the school bus.

GROUP 4–RULES FOR THE CLASSROOM

Think of as many rules as you can that should be followed in the classroom.

RULES FOR SCHOOL

Here are some appropriate rules and some inappropriate rules. Check off the appropriate rules.

GROUP 1–RULES FOR GYM CLASS

Put a checkmark beside the rules that should be followed in gym class.

___ Always wear running shoes.

___ Eat food before class.

___ Don't chew gum.

___ Listen to your gym teacher.

___ When you hear a whistle blow, stop.

___ When you hear a whistle blow, run.

___ Don't tie your laces.

___ Have fun!

GROUP 2–RULES FOR THE SCHOOLYARD

Put a checkmark beside the rules that should be followed in the schoolyard.

___ Always stay on school property during recess.

___ Don't listen to the bells and play as long as you want.

___ Take your turn on the equipment.

___ Listen to the teacher on duty.

___ Only play with your best friend and don't include other people.

___ Play safely and have fun.

RULES FOR SCHOOL

Here are appropriate rules and some inappropriate rules. Check off the appropriate rules.

GROUP 3—RULES FOR THE SCHOOL BUS

Put a checkmark beside the rules that should be followed on the school bus.

___ Sit down and don't stand up while the bus is moving.

___ Walk slowly while the bus is moving.

___ Don't talk loudly or distract the bus driver.

___ Enter the bus in single file and orderly.

___ Sit three or four people to a seat.

___ Always obey and listen to the bus driver.

GROUP 4—RULES FOR THE CLASSROOM

Put a checkmark beside the rules that should be followed in the classroom.

___ Always raise your hand when you want to speak.

___ Pass notes to friends when the teacher won't let you talk to them.

___ Always listen to your teacher.

___ Talk quietly and work well with others.

___ Keep your desk messy.

___ Keep your desk tidy.

___Treat everyone in the class with respect.

BICYCLE SAFETY CHECKLIST

Most people store their bikes inside during the winter. When you get your bike out again in the spring, here are some things you should check before riding. Use this checklist during the bike season and check your bike at least once a week.

Make sure the bike is the right size for you.
Sit on your bike and stand with your feet flat on the ground. There should be 3-8 centimetres of space between you and the top bar.

- ☐ Check the brakes to make sure they are working properly.
- ☐ Check that the tires have enough air in them.
- ☐ Oil your chain regularly.
- ☐ Tighten the seat, handlebars, and wheels.
- ☐ Make sure the wheels are straight.
- ☐ Put reflectors on the bike, so people can see you more easily.

BIKE SAFETY

Colour the picture. Draw in a bike helmet to make the girl safe.

Why is it important to wear a bike helmet?

____

____

BICYCLE SAFETY
TRUE OR FALSE QUIZ

Circle **TRUE** or **FALSE**.

1. Bicyclists do not follow the same traffic rules as cars.	**TRUE or FALSE**
2. Safe bicyclists keep their bikes in good shape.	**TRUE or FALSE**
3. Two people can ride a bike that has one seat. One person can sit on the seat and the other can sit on the handlebars.	**TRUE or FALSE**
4. Bicyclists should always wear a helmet.	**TRUE or FALSE**
5. Bicyclists should ride close to parked cars.	**TRUE or FALSE**
6. Bicyclists should never ride on the sidewalk.	**TRUE or FALSE**
7. Bicyclists should always ride their bikes across busy intersections.	**TRUE or FALSE**
8. Bicyclists should always ride on the right-hand side of the road.	**TRUE or FALSE**
9. Bicyclists should never wear a headset or a walkman when riding.	**TRUE or FALSE**
10. Bicyclists should obey all stoplights and stop signs.	**TRUE or FALSE**

BIKE RULES

Jesse is riding her bike to the park. Help Jesse make wise decisions so she has a safe ride. Check the box that shows the best answer.

1. Before Jesse gets her bike out of the garage, she should

   A. put her helmet on her head.

   B. take out the garbage.

   C. walk the dog.

2. Jesse gets her bike out of the garage and rides it down the driveway. At the end of the driveway she should

   A. wave goodbye to her mom.

   B. check for cars.

   C. pop a wheelie.

3. When Jesse leaves the driveway, she should

   A. ride on the sidewalk.

   B. ride on the street.

   C. pick up her friend.

4. Jesse comes to a stop sign. She should

   A. stop and signal which way she wants to turn.

   B. stop and pedal fast.

   C. stop and cut across traffic.

5. At the park, Jesse should

   A. lean her bike up against the fence.

   B. lay the bike on the grass so it doesn't get scratched.

   C. safely lock up her bike in a bike rack.

THE RULES OF SAFETY

- I never play outside alone. I always have a friend or family member with me.
- I know my name, address, and telephone number and my parents' names.
- I always check with my parents or someone I trust before I get into a car with anyone other than my parents.
- If someone touches me in away that I don't like, I say no.
- I tell my parents if someone touches me in a way that I don't like.
- I always check with my parents before I accept anything from a stranger or someone I don't know well.
- I know I can tell my parents anything and they will not get mad at me.
- I trust my parents.

TEACHING CHILDREN ABOUT SEXUAL ABUSE

Dear Parents and Guardians:

Below are points taken from a Children's Aid Society document. Information may be found on their Web site. (www.oacas.org)

This site helps adults teach children about sexual abuse.

- Teach children to say "no" if they don't want to be touched. This should include if they are being tickled, kissed, or hugged and don't want this.
- Teach children they have rights to privacy when it comes to dressing, bathing, or sleeping.
- Teach children that if an adult asks them to keep a secret about touching this is not okay.
- Teach children the proper names of body parts and explain to them which body parts should not be touched by adults.
- Teach children about okay touching and not okay touching and tell them they can talk to you or their parents if someone is touching them in a way that is not okay.

As a parent or guardian, you may wish to educate your child in these points.

Sincerely,

____

WHO DO YOU CALL?

You should know these phone numbers in case of an emergency.

POLICE ______________________________

FIRE ________________________________

AMBULANCE __________________________

OR YOU CAN CALL 911

911 is an emergency number. You can reach the police, fire department, and ambulance from this number.

ONLY call 911 in an emergency.

If you need to call 911,

- Tell the operator there is an emergency
- Give the operator your name and the address and where you are calling from.
- Explain what has happened. (Give as much detail as possible.)
- Stay on the line until the operator tells you to hang up.

Other numbers you may need:

KIDS HELP PHONE 1-800-668-6868

A NEIGHBOUR _________________________

Many places have block parents. Block parents are safe places for children to go in an emergency.

To find a block parent, look for the red and white sign in the window. These people will help you.

WHAT IS BULLYING?

Bullying is actions or words that harm another person.

Bullying can take many forms. It may be:

- name calling or put downs.
- physical violence.
- ignoring or excluding.

With a partner brainstorm 3 things a person who is being bullied can do.

1. ______________________________

2. ______________________________

3. ______________________________

With a partner brainstorm 2 things you can do if you see someone else being bullied.

1. ______________________________

2. ______________________________

Remember always treat others the way you would like to be treated.

Think about what makes you a good friend. Share this with a partner.

HEALTH JOURNAL

Cut out the questions. Paste the questions on another sheet of paper. Leave room for the pictures.

Cut out the pictures and paste them under the right questions.

What can you do to be safe in the sun?

What can you do to be safe in the water?

What can you do to be safe in the cold?

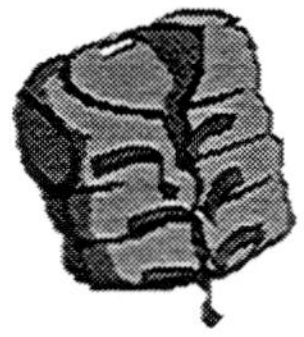
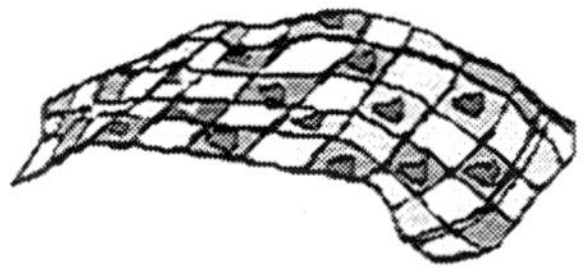

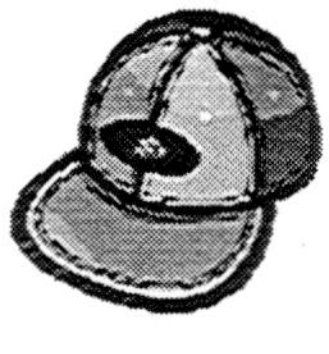

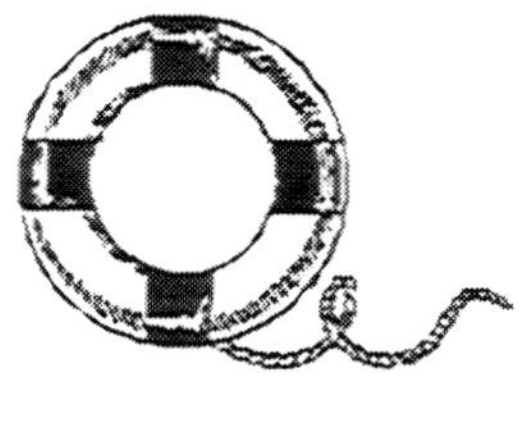

CASE STUDIES

Divide the class into four groups. Give each group one of the following cards. On each card is a situation. Each group must brainstorm ways of dealing with the situation. After they are completed, they should share their response with the class.

GROUP 1–DEALING WITH ANIMALS

Your friend just got a dog. She thinks it is funny to pull its tail. She doesn't know how to treat the dog because she has never had a dog before.

Tell your friend how a dog should be treated.

GROUP 2–AT THE MALL

At the mall with your Mom, you get lost. What would you do?

GROUP 3–AT THE POOL

Your friend has a swimming pool in his backyard. You are over playing with him when he suggests you jump in the pool. There are no adults around. You both jump in. Suddenly, your friend is having trouble swimming and yells for help. What would you do?

GROUP 4–IN THE WOODS

Your house is near a wooded area. Even though you are not allowed to play in the woods alone, you go anyway. After a few hours you realize you are lost. What would you do?

WHAT TO DO IN AN EMERGENCY

READ THE FOLLOWING:

An emergency can be scary because it is serious and you don't have lots of time to plan how you will react. In an emergency, you can call 911 if it is serious enough that you need the police, fire department, or an ambulance. If you are not near a phone, scream 'help!' as loud as you can.

In an emergency, try not to panic. This won't help the situation. If the person cannot move, do not move the person. The person may have a neck injury and moving him/her could be very dangerous.

Finally, do not try to be a superhero and save someone's life. Trying to save a person from drowning or rescuing someone from a burning building is dangerous. You could end up getting hurt or worse being killed yourself. Trying to rescue someone may make it even harder for police or firefighters to do their job.

Be calm! Be brave! And know that help will arrive soon!

WHAT TO DO IN AN EMERGENCY

After reading the information, use the words to fill the blanks.

911	superhero	emergency	Scary	help
panic	killed	neck	Ambulance	aid

An emergency can be ____________________ because it is serious and you don't have lots of time to plan how you will react. In an ____________________________, you can call ________________ if it is serious enough that you need the police, fire department, or an __________________________. If you are not near a phone, scream '___________________!' as loud as you can.

In an emergency, try not to _____________________. This won't help the situation. If the person cannot move, do not move the person. The person may have a ___________injury and moving him/her could be very dangerous. Finally, do not try to be a __________________ and save someone's life. Trying to save a person from drowning or rescuing someone from a burning building is dangerous. You could end up getting hurt or worse being ___________________ yourself. Trying to rescue someone may make it even harder for police or firefighters to do their job.

Be calm! Be brave! And know that help will arrive soon!

SAFETY BOOKMARK ASSIGNMENT

You have learned lots about safety in this unit. For this assignment, you will create a safety bookmark. On your bookmark, you will write two rules (one for each side) or things a person should think about in order to be safe.

Your bookmark might be about safety in a specific situation (like in the water or sun) or about safety in general.

After you have written your rule, colour your bookmark.

PERSONAL SAFETY & INJURY PREVENTION

SAFETY BOOKMARK RUBRIC

CRITERIA	LEVEL 1	LEVEL 2	LEVEL 3	LEVEL 4
Knowledge	- has a limited knowledge of safety rules	- has some knowledge of safety rules	- has good knowledge of safety rules	- has excellent knowledge of safety rules
Creativity	- the bookmark lacks any creativity	- the bookmark shows limited creativity	- the bookmark has some creativity	-the bookmark demonstrates excellent creativity
Proofreading	- so many language errors it is difficult to read the bookmark	- lots of language errors that sometimes makes it difficult to read the bookmark	- some language errors, but errors don't take away from meaning	- very few language errors

ADDITIONAL COMMENTS

____

____

____

____

____

____

THE SAFETY PLEDGE

Note to Teacher—Have your class take "The Safety Pledge." All the students should stand beside their desk and put their right hand on their heart and their left hand in the air as if taking an oath.

Read the pledge aloud one line at a time and have students repeat the line in unison.

I ______________________________ (state your name) promise to help a friend in need or a person who is being bullied.

I promise never to bully others and to treat everyone as I would like to be treated.

I promise never to hurt anyone either with words or hands.

I promise if I am bullied that I will ignore the bully or seek help from an adult.

I promise to always tell my parents where I am when I play outside, and I will never play outside alone.

I promise never to get into a car of a stranger or someone other than my parents without my parents knowing.

I promise to live safely, to plan a fire escape at home and at school, and to always look both ways before crossing the street.

I promise to always wear a helmet when I ride a bike and to obey the rules of the road.

I promise to always play sports safely.

I promise to always tell my parents if something is bothering me or if I don't like how someone is touching me or treating me.

FIRST AID WORDS

These words have something to do with first aid.
Learn the words and then find them in the word search.

Bandaid—covers a wound or a cut.

Cast—a hard, protective wrapping that goes around the area near a broken bone to keep the bone in place.

Dislocation—what happens when a bone gets pulled out of its joint.

Fracture—a break in a bone.

Frostbite—damage to the skin or body parts that are exposed to freezing cold temperatures.

Heat Stroke—when your body gets too hot.

Ice—used to cool down an injury or swelling.

Shock—when your body isn't getting oxygen where it needs.

Stitches—doctors use a thread-like material to sew together serious cuts.

B	A	P	T	R	O	V	B	K	F	M	N	I	C	E
A	R	E	I	K	V	B	D	J	R	L	O	P	H	S
N	Q	U	S	C	A	S	T	U	O	W	Z	A	C	F
D	G	H	K	B	N	P	R	R	S	E	L	R	C	M
A	Z	W	R	T	Y	U	I	O	T	P	A	S	D	F
I	G	H	J	K	L	Z	X	C	B	V	B	N	M	S
D	X	T	Y	P	O	I	E	C	I	L	J	Y	H	R
W	R	T	U	K	T	R	X	C	T	V	B	O	N	M
A	I	F	D	L	U	X	C	V	E	B	C	M	A	Z
W	I	Y	K	T	D	C	V	M	N	K	S	W	E	A
S	E	H	C	T	I	T	S	Y	B	N	L	T	K	B
Q	W	A	E	R	R	Y	U	I	O	P	A	S	D	F
G	R	H	E	A	T	S	T	R	O	K	E	E	R	T
F	Y	U	I	N	O	I	T	A	C	O	L	S	I	D

P-A-S-T-E:
A WAY TO SOLVE PROBLEMS

When you have a problem, you may want to think of P-A-S-T-E. This is a way to come up with a solution to your problems. P-A-S-T-E stands for the following:

P—stands for PROBLEM
Ask yourself what the problem is.

A—stands for ALTERNATIVE
Alternative means another way. Think about different ways of dealing with the problem.

S—stands for SOLUTION
From your alternatives, decide a solution to the problem.

T—stands for TRY
Try the solution to your problem.

E—stands for EVALUATE
Evaluate the success of your solution.

Imagine that you really want to go to the park to play on the swings. Your Mom doesn't want you to go alone. Your Mom can't go with you because she's wallpapering the living room. Use P-A-S-T-E to solve this problem. Write your ideas here:

____

____

____

____

____

____

WHAT TO DO ...

WHAT TO DO IF YOU GET THE FLU:

1. Get lots of sleep. Even if you're not tired, lie in bed and read or relax
2. Drink lots of fluids, especially water
3. Wash your hands so you don't spread the germs.
4. Wear layers of clothing because you'll probably be cold one minute and hot the next.
5. Only take medication if your parents feel you need it.
6. If you can keep food down, eat bland, dry foods like plain toast.

WHAT TO DO IF YOU GET A BEE STING:

1. Tell an adult right away. A few people are allergic to bee stings, and you will need help if you are.
2. Ask the adult to remove the stinger.
3. Wash the bite with soap and water.
4. Hold an ice cube against the bite for about 10 minutes or until the swelling goes down.

WHAT TO DO IF YOU GET A NOSEBLEED:

1. Sit down and lean forward. (not back)
2. Place a cold wet cloth on your nose and press firmly on the nostrils. If this hurts, don't press as hard. Keep the cloth there for about 10 minutes.
3. Don't blow your nose for a while because this will cause your nose to bleed again.

PERSONAL SAFETY & INJURY PREVENTION QUIZ

Circle true or false.

1. If you get a nosebleed always lean your head back.	TRUE or FALSE
2. Always wear running shoes in gym class.	TRUE or FALSE
3. It's okay for kids to ride a bike and not wear a helmet as long as they are riding on the sidewalk.	TRUE or FALSE
4. Bicyclists follow the same rules as cars.	TRUE or FALSE
5. People can call 9-1-1 in an emergency.	TRUE or FALSE
6. Bullying includes name-calling as well as physical violence.	TRUE or FALSE
7. To be safe in the sun a person should drink water and wear a hat and sunscreen.	TRUE or FALSE
8. If someone is drowning, you should risk your own life to try and save that person.	TRUE or FALSE
9. Frostbite may occur when your body is exposed to extreme heat.	TRUE or FALSE
10. Shock is when your body isn't getting the oxygen to where it needs it.	TRUE or FALSE

PERSONAL SAFETY AND INJURY PREVENTION CERTIFICATE

Congratulations!

____

You have completed the
personal safety and injury prevention unit.

Great Work!

Personal Safety and Injury Prevention Reflection Journal

Name: ____________________

The part I liked best about this unit was........

____

Two things I learned ....

1. ______________________________________

2. ______________________________________

UNIT 5: SELF ESTEEM & PERSONAL RELATIONSHIPS

In this unit, students will learn how they express certain emotions. There are tips for making friends. Students will be encouraged to think about important people in their lives, to examine ways of solving conflicts, and to learn more about their friends and classmates. Stereotypes of boys and girls will also be discussed. Ideas about how to help out at home will be examined. Students will learn various aspects of what makes them unique by creating "A Book About Me!"

The purpose of this unit is to allow students to explore themselves and feel proud of whom they are and the talents they have. There is no quiz at the end of the unit. This unit does not consist of facts but allows students to explore themselves.

HEALTH JOURNAL

I am happy when ...
I am sad when ...
I am mad when ...

TIPS FOR MAKING AND KEEPING FRIENDS

- ♥ Be a good listener
- ♥ Support and encourage your friends
- ♥ Share with your friends
- ♥ Be kind
- ♥ Laugh together
- ♥ Respect your friends
- ♥ Play fair

I have a friend. My friend's name is

____.

He/She is a good friend because

____

____

THE IMPORTANT PEOPLE IN YOUR LIFE

We all have people who are very important to us. These people might be our parents, other family members, or close friends. In this activity, you will choose five people who are important to you. Write their names in the left-hand column on the chart. For each person write one point telling why this person is important to you.

NAME OF PERSON	WHY THIS PERSON IS IMPORTANT TO YOU

THE HIGHS AND LOWS IN LIFE

Everyone has highs and lows. The highs are the times that make us excited. They might be things like passing a test or learning how to ride a bike.

People also have lows. These are the times that make us sad or upset. They might be things like having a fight with your brother or sister or having a pet die.

Think about the times in your life when you have felt really good. Make a list of them here:

Think about the times in your life when you have felt bad. Make a list of them here:

WHAT WOULD YOU DO?

Sometimes people don't get along with each other or they have problems with their friends. Here are different situations where a person is having trouble with a group of people. Read each situation and decide what you would do to help the person.

Situation 1

A new student named Dzuy has come to Canada and joined your class. Dzuy doesn't speak any English. Your teacher has asked everyone to help Dzuy fit in, but some students are mean to him and tease him. You notice that he doesn't play with anyone at recess or lunch and is always alone. What would you do to help Dzuy?

____

____

____

____

Situation 2

Your friend, Carla, gets a new bike in the spring. Two weeks later, her parents buy her a TV. No one else has a TV. Carla brags about her bike and TV so much that people stop speaking to her. Very soon, Carla has no friends. You want to be nice to Carla but the other students in the class tell you they'll stop speaking to you if you are nice to Carla. What would you do to help Carla?

____

____

____

____

WHAT WOULD YOU DO?

Sometimes people don't get along with each other or they have problems with their friends. Here are different situations where a person is having trouble with a group of people. Read each situation and decide what you would do to help the person.

SITUATION 3

You and your best friend, Chris, are in the school play. The director, Mr. Wu, has asked the students in the play to help write it. You share your ideas with Chris. Then, without telling you, she shares the ideas with Mr. Wu. She tells him that they are her ideas. He thinks they are brilliant and plans to use them in the play. You are very angry with Chris. How do you think you should handle the situation?

____

____

____

____

SITUATION 4

You see a boy named Doug in your class take a pen off the teacher's desk. When she asks for it, Doug doesn't say anything. A few days later, you see him take some food from someone's lunch bag. Again, the person asks about it, but Doug doesn't come clean. Then, a student from the class is missing an expensive jacket. You think Doug might have taken it, but you don't have any proof. How would you handle this situation?

____

____

____

____

WAYS OF RESOLVING CONFLICTS WITH YOUR FRIENDS

- ➢ Talk it out
- ➢ Do not act violently
- ➢ Put yourself in the other person's shoes
- ➢ Don't lose your temper
- ➢ Listen to both sides of the argument
- ➢ Come up with solutions together
- ➢ Learn to forgive and forget

****

When I had a problem with a friend, we solved the problem by

____

____

____

____

WHAT ARE YOUR RESPONSIBILITIES AT HOME?

Show the people you live with how much you appreciate all the things they do by helping out around the house.

Below are coupons for jobs that you can do to help out at home. Cut the coupons out and take them home. Surprise your caregiver with the coupon and then complete the job.

ONE FREE COUPON

for ___________________________

I promise to make my bed.

ONE FREE COUPON

for ___________________________

I promise to put my toys away.

ONE FREE COUPON

for ___________________________

I promise to put my clothes away after I get ready for bed.

ONE FREE COUPON

for ___________________________

I promise to put the dishes away after they have been cleaned.

WHAT ARE YOUR RESPONSIBILITIES AT HOME?

Show the people you live with how much you appreciate all the things they do by helping out around the house.

Below are coupons for jobs that you can do to help out at home. Cut the coupons out and take them home. Surprise your caregiver with the coupon and then complete the job.

ONE FREE COUPON

for ______________________________

I promise to wash the dishes or put them in the dishwasher.

ONE FREE COUPON

for ______________________________

I promise to set the table.

ONE FREE COUPON

for ______________________________

I promise to sweep the kitchen floor.

ONE FREE COUPON

for ______________________________

I promise to wipe the kitchen counter after dinner is made.

STEREOTYPES OF BOYS AND GIRLS

The word stereotype means "an idea that many people have about a thing or group that may be untrue or only partly true."

For example, some people who don't live in Canada think Canadians live in igloos and that it snows here all year. Although we do get a lot of snow, this is not quite true and is a stereotype about life in Canada.

Many people have stereotypes about boys and girls. The problem with stereotypes is that people sometimes accept the stereotypes and then they act differently to make the stereotypes come true.

Think of THREE stereotypes people have about boys. List them below.

1. ____

2. ____

3. ____

Think of THREE stereotypes people have about girls. List them below.

1. ____

2. ____

3. ____

What is the worst stereotype for either boys or girls? Explain why you feel this way.

____

____

____

THE STORY OF YOUR NAME

Every name has a story behind it. What is the story behind your name? You may want to ask your parents for help when you complete this worksheet.

What is your first name?

____

What is the story behind your first name?

____

____

____

What is your middle name?

____

What is the story behind your middle name?

____

____

____

What is your last name?

____

Where is this name from? Is there any interesting story about the history of your last name or other people who share the same last name?

WHERE DO YOU LIVE?

In what town/city do you live?

____

What do you like about living here?

____

____

____

In what country do you live?

____

What do you like about living in this country?

____

____

____

Except for Canada's First Nations people, everyone in Canada moved here from another country.
What country did your family live in before coming to Canada?

____

When did your family move to Canada? Why did they come here?

____

____

____

A FAMILY TREE

Complete this family tree.

Your Mom's Mom	Your Mom's Dad	Your Dad's Mom	Your Dad's Dad
(name)	(name)	(name)	(name)

Your Mom	Your Dad
(name)	(name)

You
(name)

Add the names of any brothers and sisters below.

HEALTH JOURNAL

1. What can you do to be a good child to your caregivers?

2. What can you do to be a good brother or sister?

3. What can you do to be a good person to older people?

4. What can you do to be a good neighbour?

LETTER TO PARENTS
HOME STUDY

Dear Parent(s) or Guardian(s):

For the final health assignment, your child will be creating "A Book About Me." The purpose of this book is to help build your child's self esteem by celebrating his/her talents and what makes him/her unique.

The book is divided into 7 chapters.

Chapter 1—In the Beginning

Chapter 2—The Facts and Nothing But the Facts

Chapter 3—My Likes and Dislikes

Chapter 4—The People in My Life

Chapter 5—My Talents and Interests

Chapter 6—Life at School

Chapter 7—My Future

Attached are the blank pages of the book. Please help your child complete these pages. Your child may also want to add photos or other pictures.

The book must be completed by ____________________________.

If you have any questions about this assignment, please contact me directly.

Sincerely,

____

A BOOK ABOUT ME!

This is a portrait of me.

By

CHAPTER 1 –IN THE BEGINNING!

My full name is ______________________________

____

My date of birth is ______________________________

____

My parents' names are ______________________________

____

The hospital where I was born is ______________________________

____

The town/city where I was born is ______________________________

____

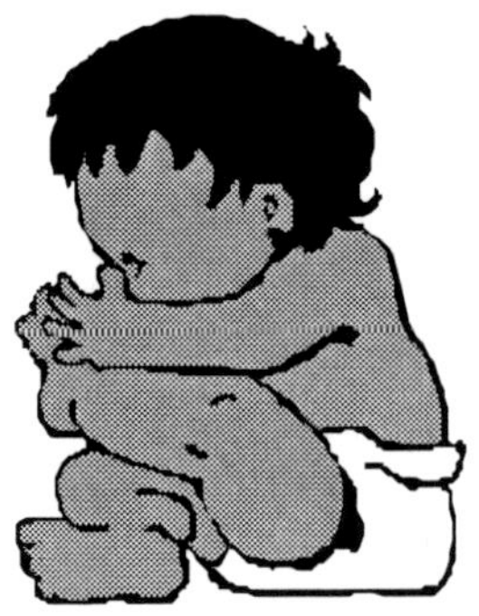

CHAPTER 2–THE FACTS AND NOTHING BUT THE FACTS!

This is what I look like...

My eye colour is

____

My hair colour is

____

My skin colour is

____

My height is

____

My weight is

____

Something special about me is

____

____

(An example for the above is—I look different than anyone else because I have three freckles on my nose.)

CHAPTER 3–
MY LIKES AND DISLIKES

Below is a chart. In the middle column is a list of categories. For each category choose something you like and something you don't like. Write each of these items in the chart.

For example, if the category is food, you may like pizza and you may dislike mushrooms, so your chart would look like this:

LIKES	CATEGORY	DISLIKES
Pizza	FOOD	Mushrooms

Complete the chart by adding your likes and dislikes.

LIKES	CATEGORY	DISLIKES
	FOOD	
	TOYS	
	MOVIES OR TV SHOWS	
	SPORTS	
	BOOKS	

Choose one category and explain WHY you like what you picked and why you dislike what you picked.

Category ____________________ Like ____________________

Why____

Category ____________________ Dislike ____________________

Why____

CHAPTER 4–THE PEOPLE IN MY LIFE

There are many people in your life who are special. Complete the chart by listing the names of the people in your life. In the second column write one reason this person is special to you.

PERSON	REASON THIS PERSON IS SPECIAL
Mom (name)____________________	
Dad (name)____________________	
Brother or Sister (name)____________________	
Brother or Sister (name)____________________	
Dad's Dad (Your Grandpa) (name)____________________	
Dad's Mom (Your Grandma) (name)____________________	
Mom's Dad (Your Grandpa) (name)____________________	
Mom's Mom (Your Grandma) (name)____________________	
A Special Friend (name)____________________	
A Special Friend (name)____________________	
Your Pet (name)____________________	

CHAPTER 5–MY TALENTS AND INTERESTS

List five things that you are proud of. For example, you might be proud of winning a ribbon at track and field day or learning how to ride a bike.

1. ______________________________

2. ______________________________

3. ______________________________

4. ______________________________

5. ______________________________

List three activities you participate in.

1. ______________________________

2. ______________________________

3. ______________________________

A talent is something you are very good at. For example, you might have a talent as a singer or a hockey player. Think of your talents. List three of them below.

1. ______________________________

2. ______________________________

3. ______________________________

CHAPTER 6–LIFE AT SCHOOL

Name of Your School ______________________________

What grade are you in? ______________________________

Teacher's Name ______________________________

What is your favourite memory from this grade?

____

____

Who were your teachers before this year?

____

____

List three things you like about your school

1. ______________________________

2. ______________________________

3. ______________________________

CHAPTER 7–MY FUTURE

Twenty-five years is a long way away. How old will you be in 25 years? In the space below, predict where you will be and what will have happened to you and what you will be doing.

____

____

____

Draw a picture of how you will look like in 25 years.

SELF ESTEEM & PERSONAL RELATIONSHIPS

ALL ABOUT ME BOOK RUBRIC

CRITERIA	LEVEL 1	LEVEL 2	LEVEL 3	LEVEL 4
Completion of Assignment	Completed one or two of the chapters for *A Book About Me!*	Completed three or four of the chapters for *A Book About Me!*	Completed five or six of the chapters for *A Book About Me!*	Completed all seven of the chapters for *A Book About Me!*
Organization	- had lots of difficulty writing the material in the graphic organizers and charts and completing the activity sheets.	- had some difficulty writing the material in the graphic organizers and charts and completing the activity sheets.	- had no difficulty writing the material in the graphic organizers and charts and completing the activity sheets.	- wrote the material in the graphic organizers and charts and completed the activity sheets. in a superb manner.
Proofreading	- so many language errors it is difficult to understand text	- lots of language errors that sometimes makes it difficult to understand text	- some language errors, but errors don't take away from meaning	- very few language errors
Level of Assistance (information required from parents)	- lots of adult resistance was required	- some adult assistance was required	- little adult assistance was required	- no adult assistance was required

ADDITIONAL COMMENTS

____

____

____

____

Congratulations!

You have completed
the Personal Relationships and
Self-Esteem unit.

Great Work!

Personal Relationships Name: ____________________

And Self-Esteem

Reflection Journal

The part I liked best about this unit was........

____

Two things I learned ....

1. ____

2. ____

UNIT 6: PHYSICAL ACTIVITY

In this unit, students will examine why exercise makes them healthy, how to play certain games, different sports people play, and examine their own exercise routines.

HELPFUL HINTS

Studies show that children are in the worst shape in history. Since students are often not participating in sports and getting exercise at home, it is more important than ever for teachers to include physical activity in their schedule. It isn't as important for students to learn structured lessons about specific sports as it is for them to get active. This means don't worry about whether or not they can successfully put a basketball in a net as much as you should have students running around in an organized activity that gets them in shape.

Make this unit fun! There are many games that students can play that are fun and help them get exercise at the same time. If you are not sure what games to play, visit your local library. Most libraries have a great collection of game books.

CULMINATING ACTIVITY

In this unit, students will participate in a challenge that encourages them to get in shape and avoid TV, the phone, and the computer.

WHY SHOULD YOU EXERCISE?

Exercise is good for you. It makes your body healthy. It gives you strong muscles. It can make you happy. Your heart pumps faster when you exercise and this is good for your heart. It makes your heart strong. Exercise every day because, exercise makes you healthy!

Cut out the pictures and put them in the right spaces.

1. Exercise gives you strong __________________.

2. Exercise makes your ________________________ pump faster.

3. Exercise makes you ______________________.

4. Exercise makes you ______________________.

WHAT SPORTS DO PEOPLE PLAY?

Fill in the chart. Think about the sports people play.

List all the winter sports you can think of.	List all the summer sports you can think of.

List all the indoor sports you can think of.	List all the outdoor sports you can think of.

List all the team sports you can think of.	List all the individual sports you can think of.

GAMES FOR STUDENTS

Many grades 1-3 students lack coordination necessary for many sports. Playing games is a great way to help them get exercise. Here are a few games you may wish to play with your students to get them moving and staying in shape:

1. **Marco Polo**—The objective of this game is not to get caught by "Marco." One person who is "it" closes his eyes and wears a blindfold. The rest of the class avoids this person. When the person who is "it" shouts, "Marco," the other people shout, "Polo." This helps the person who is "it" determine where the others are. If he touches a person, that person becomes it.

2. **British Bulldog**—The class stands at one end of a field with one person, who is "it" standing in the middle of the field. When the person in the middle yells out "British Bulldog," the students run across the field trying to get to the other side. If these students get touched by the person who is "it," they join this person in the middle and help her try to catch the others.

3. **Catch the Dragon's Tail**—Make a chain of 6 to 8 students. (They can hold the waist of the person ahead of them.) The student at the end of the chain has a scarf tucked into his pants at the waist. The student at the front of the chain will run around trying to grab the scarf, while the person wearing the scarf tries to avoid this from happening.

4. **What Time Is It, Mr. Wolf**—One player is the Wolf and stands at the end of the field with her back to the others. The others call out, "What time is it, Mr. Wolf?" The wolf picks a time—for example, 10 o'clock. This means the players take 10 steps towards the wolf. If the wolf yells, "Dinner time!" the players run back to the end of the field. Any player caught by the wolf becomes the wolf.

CULMINATING ACTIVITY:
A PHYSICAL ACTIVITY CHALLENGE

Dear Parents and Guardians,

Studies show that children today watch an increasing amount of TV and spend too much time on the computer or talking on the phone. These types of activities keep students from getting exercise. The Home Physical Activity Challenge encourages children to get away from the TV, the phone, and the computer for a week in order to get into shape.

WEEK 1

Using the Physical Activity Challenge Recording Sheet with your child, keep track and calculate how many hours are spent

- watching TV
- on the phone
- using the computer.

WEEK 2

Promote physical activity by having your child do a physical activity for every hour spent the previous week watching TV, on the computer, or talking on the phone. During the second week encourage your child to spend less time doing inactive activities.

HELPFUL HINT......

Discuss with your child that physical activity includes more than just traditional exercise or sport. For example, raking leaves, walking the dog, shoveling snow, and vacuuming are all activities that can help someone get into shape.

Your participation in our physical activity challenge is greatly appreciated.

Kind regards,

____

PHYSICAL ACTIVITY CHALLENGE
WEEK ONE

Day	Watching T.V.	Talking on the phone	On the computer.
Monday			
Tuesday			
Wednesday			
Thursday			
Friday			
Total Hours			

PHYSICAL ACTIVITY CHALLENGE
WEEK TWO

How does exercise make you feel?

____

What is your favourite type of exercise?

____

PHYSICAL ACTIVITY CHALLENGE
WEEK TWO

Over five days, look at how much you exercise each day. In the chart, write down all the exercise you have done in a day. Make sure you include things like walking to school or playing games with your friends.
After completing the chart answer the questions in the "Examine Your Exercise Routines—Journal."

Day of the Week	Exercise You Did
Day 1	
Day 2	
Day 3	
Day 4	
Day 5	

PHYSICAL ACTIVITY CHALLENGE REFLECTION JOURNAL

Read the questions.
To answer the questions, circle **NEVER**, **SOMETIMES**, or **OFTEN**.

1. Do you get at least an hour of exercise every day?

NEVER SOMETIMES ALWAYS

2. Do you participate in organized sports?

NEVER SOMETIMES ALWAYS

3. Do you participate in sports and exercise activities with your family?

NEVER SOMETIMES ALWAYS

Answer the questions.

1. What sport do you enjoy playing or doing the most?

____

2. What activities and sports do you play with your family?

____

3. Do you think you get enough exercise every day? YES or NO? Explain your answer.

____

____

____

____

FIVE MINUTE CIRCUIT

Cut out the ten boxes and spread them out on the wall around your gym. Have your students complete the circuit by moving from one station to the next. Have no more than 4 students at one station at a time. Do this circuit once a week all year and your students will eventually notice an improvement. Time 30-seconds and blow a whistle after 30-seconds is up indicating students must move to the next station.

Circuit 1—Jump a skipping rope for 30 seconds.

Circuit 2—Bounce a basketball up and down with two hands for 30 seconds.

Circuit 3—Do as many jumping jacks as you can for 30 seconds.

Circuit 4—Jump up and down on two feet and touch a spot on the wall for 30 seconds.

Circuit 5—Lean your back against the wall, bend your knees, and pretend you are sitting in a chair. Hold this position for 30 seconds.

Circuit 6—Sit on the floor with your legs straight out. Try to touch your toes. Hold this position for 30 seconds.

Circuit 7—Throw a volleyball against the wall. Let the ball bounce on the floor once and catch it. Do this for 30 seconds.

Circuit 8—Run through a zigzag series of pylons for 30 seconds.

(Your teacher will set up the pylons.)

Circuit 9—Walk across a balance beam, a bench, or a line and back again for 30 seconds. (Your teacher will set up the beam or bench.)

Circuit 10—Do as many burpies as you can for 30 seconds. (Burpies include jumping in the air. Go down into a push-up position and jump into a squat.)

MODIFYING SPORTS

Many elementary students lack the coordination skills to play traditional sports. Thus, you may wish to introduce traditional sports by modifying them slightly so that students feel some success. Here are some examples of how you can modify traditional sports.

FRISBEE GOLF

Set up a golf course in the schoolyard. Spread a series of 10 pylons throughout the field. Put a number on each pylon. The pylons are the "holes." Each student will need a Frisbee. The object of this sport is for students to throw their Frisbees as close to the pylon as possible. They can keep track of how many times it takes them for their Frisbee to hit the pylon. Students can go through the course in groups of 4.

BEACH BALL VOLLEYBALL

Set up a volleyball net with 6 players on each side. Instead of using a real volleyball, students can play with a beach ball instead. Each side can hit the beach ball (but not catch it) as many times as possible before getting it over the net. If the beach ball hits the ground, then the team loses control of the ball and the opposing team gets a point.

SOCCER BASEBALL

Like baseball, set up the three bases and home plate. One team of students is in the outfield and the other is "at bat." The pitcher has a soccer ball instead of a baseball. The pitcher rolls the soccer ball to the person at bat. The person at bat kicks the soccer ball and then runs to first base. The outfield can catch the ball with their hands or kick it to the first base person, who is trying to tag the runner. Like baseball, the players get three strikes and three outs.

BASKETBALL HOCKEY

This is basically the game of basketball although the students are trying to get the ball into a hockey net instead of a basketball net. Some students also have trouble dribbling a basketball, so you may wish to use a volleyball instead. Students can dribble with two hands or one. They may also throw the ball from one player to the next to move it down the court. Students cannot take more than two steps with the ball. Students get two points every time the volleyball gets in the hockey net.

T-BALL

Instead of traditional baseball, have students hit the ball off a T-stand. If your school doesn't own such a stand, you may try to borrow one from your local community centre.

PHYSICAL ACTIVITY CERTIFICATE

Congratulations!

____

You have completed the
Physical Activity Unit

Great Work!

Physical Activity Name: ____________________

Reflection Journal

The part I liked best about this unit was........

____

Two things I learned ....

1. ______________________________

2. ______________________________

RELATED WEB SITES

Kids Health.org This is an amazing site that covers a huge range of health-related topics.
www.kidshealth.org

Safe Kids Canada This site provides teachers and parents with information to help keep kids safe.
www.safekids.canada

An anti-bullying site This is a great site providing information on bullying.
www.bullying.org

Stay alert...Stay Safe This site is from Canada's leading streetproofing program for kids ages 7-10.
www.sass.ca

The First Aid Quiz A fun first aid quiz for students.
www.firstaidquiz.com

The Lung Association of Canada, Especially for Children
www.lung.ca/children

The Lung Association of Canada, Especially for Teachers
www.lung.ca/teachers

Healthy Choices for Kids Online This is a nutrition education program created by the growers of Washington State Apples.

www.healthy choices.org

The American Dental Hygenists' Association, Kids Stuff
This site provides activities for kids around dentail health
www.adha.org/kidstuff

Health Canada: a site for kids

A great site from Health Canada the includes information for kids on smoking, alcohol, drugs, food, safety and much more.

http://www.hc-sc.gc.ca/english/for_you/kids.html

ANSWERS

Unit 1: Healthy Eating

HEALTHY EATING QUIZ

Check marks should go beside the following healthy foods 2, 4, 5, 7, 8, 9, and 11.

WHAT IS CAFFEINE?

1. A. Caffeine is a drug found in coffee beans, tea-leaves, cacao, and cola nuts.
   B. Caffeine helps make people more awake.
   C. Lots of caffeine may make a person's heart pump faster and they may breathe faster.
   D. Caffeine can also make people go to the bathroom.

2. It make people's heart pump faster, it makes people breathe faster, it makes people have trouble sleeping, and it makes people more awake.

3. A person might get shaky, headaches, or stomach aches.

4. Water, milk, or juice.

Unit 2: Substance Use & Abuse

COMPARING NICOTINE AND ALCOHOL

	NICOTINE	ALCOHOL
What is it?	This is a highly addictive drug found in tobacco and smoked in cigarettes	This is a legal drug found in beer, wine, and some other beverages.
What are the short-term affects of this drug?	- bad breath - costs lots of money - yellow skin - cough	- slurred speech - loss of balance - blurry vision - may throw up or pass out
What are the long-term affects of this drug?	- higher chance of getting colds, pneumonia or serious diseases such as lung cancer	- permanent nerve, liver, or brain damage - may cause serious diseases such as cancer of the stomach

ANSWERS

SUSTANCE USE AND ABUSE TRUE/FALSE QUIZ

1. False	**2. True**
3. True	**4. False**
5. True	**6. True**
7. False	**8. True**
9. False	**10. True**

Unit 3: Growth and Development

LEARN ABOUT THE LIFE CYCLE OF PEOPLE

(6) teenage, (2) birth, (7) adult, (1) baby in the womb, (5) young child, (3) newborn baby, (8) death, (4) toddler

WHAT ARE GERMS (QUESTIONS)?

1. Germs are tiny, invisible, living organisms that can sometimes cause diseases.
2. Two types of germs are bacteria and viruses.
3. Bacteria can cause strep throat, cavities, and pneumonia.
4. Viruses can cause the flu, measles, and chicken pox.
5. Bacteria is different from viruses because it can live outside living cells.
6. The main way to protect yourself from germs is to wash your hands with soap and warm water. You can also cover your mouth when you sneeze or cough to stop spreading your germs.

TRUE/FALSE QUIZ FOR THE GROWTH AND DEVELOPMENT UNIT

1. true	2. false
3. true	4. true
5. false	6. true
7. true	8. true
9. false	10. true

ANSWERS

Unit 4: Personal Safety and Injury Prevention

BICYCLE SAFETY TEST

1. false- bicycles and cars should follow the same traffic rules.	2. true
3. false- two people should never ride the same bike	4. true
5. false- bicyclists should avoid riding too close to parked cars because a door might open suddenly.	6. true
7. false-bicyclists should always walk their bikes across busy intersections.	8. true
9. true	10. true

BIKE RULES

1. Before Jesse gets her bike out of the garage, she should put her helmet on her head.
2. Jesse gets her bike out of the garage and rides it down the driveway. At the end of the driveway she should check for cars.
3. When Jesse leaves the driveway, she should ride on the street.
4. Jesse comes to a stop sign. She should stop and signal which way she wants to turn.
5. At the park, Jesse should safely lock up her bike in a bike rack.

WHAT IS BULLYING?

Although the answers will vary, here are some sample answers you can share with your class.

With a partner brainstorm 3 things a person who is being bullied can do.

1. Tell an adult
2. Write down what has happened
3. Try to stay calm
4. Try to ignore the bully
5. Tell the bully to stop
6. Stand up. Don't stand back
7. Join a club or team and try to make new friends.

ANSWERS

WHAT IS BULLYING? Cont'd

With a partner brainstorm 2 things you can do if you see someone else being bullied.

1. Don't join in.
2. Help the kid who is being bullied by leading him away from the bully.
3. Don't make the bully feel important by paying attention to him.
4. Befriend the person who is being bullied.
5. Encourage the kid who is being bullied to tell an adult.

WHAT TO DO IN AN EMERGENCY

An emergency can be scary because it is serious and you don't have lots of time to plan how you will react. In an emergency, you can call 911 if it is serious enough that you need the police, fire department, or an ambulance. If you are not near a phone, scream 'help!' as loud as you can.

In an emergency, try not to panic. This won't help the situation. If the person cannot move, do not move the person. The person may have a neck injury and moving him/her could be very dangerous.

Finally, do not try to be a superhero and save someone's life. Trying to save a person from drowning or rescuing someone from a burning building is dangerous. You could end up getting hurt or worse being killed yourself. Trying to rescue someone may make it even harder for police or firefighters to do their job.

Be calm! Be brave! And know that help will arrive soon!

FIRST AID WORDS AND THE WORD SEARCH

B									F			I	C	E
A									R					
N				C	A	S	T		O					
D									S					
A									T					
I									B					S
D							E		I				H	
						R			T			O		
					U				E		C			
				T						K				
S	E	H	C	T	I	T	S							
		A												
	R	H	E	A	T	S	T	R	O	K	E			
F				N	O	I	T	A	C	O	L	S	I	D

ANSWERS

PERSONAL SAFETY AND INJURY PREVENTION QUIZ

1. false	2. true
3. false	4. true
5. true	6. true
7. true	8. false
9. false	10. true